The
DAILY
CANDY
LEXICON

COUNTING TERROR aim APATHY HOUR bad reception-ist BLUETOOTHSO
ONFERENCE CRAWL desk burn E-MAUL golden paratrooper MEGO messenger
MS phone zit PROMOTION SICKNESS reply-arrhea SUPER CASUAL FRIDAY
? WISHFUL DRINKING altarcation AM-BUSHED amoraphobia BLUE BALLSY
ONDAMN cunnalinguist DEBAUCHELOR dizo FLACID ghag GUYATUS headhu
ebridate LADY BUSINESS CASUAL locationship MAID OF DISHONOR manbig
ASTURFAKER nuptualpalooza PDR rockafella SCOODGE scum SNOOPID vir(tu
HITE RUSSIAN ROULETTE whor d'oeuvre BRATKINS bro yo CARB BOMB carb
otprint CEREAL MONOGAMY crappuccino CRAPAS foodilicious FRUCT UP gru
AITRESS ickymaki KITCHEN AID marshmellow MARTYRINI mean cuisine OF
NIC pst RAWFUL salad spinster SCHLOCKTAIL sharon von munchausen SINAE
oitan SPAMMELIER tart fuel TASTY DE-LIE tripe-idation ACHILLES HEEL an
SDRESS dressausage DRESSING TOMB fabric-ation FEARRORS flee market GO
DGET ARM inshopnia MOOSE HOOF mouse trap REFLECTION PERIOD ripta
AUL pharmasecrecy SANDBAG skew-tique SHOPPINGS un-modest mouse VIVI
ARD wwkd AMATEUR NIGHT OWL collateral DANCE DANCE EVOLUTION dr
ll FLEETING fridea INTOXICANTILEVER lush flush MARGARITER nontoura
ohographer PTPD pui REHOUNDING restaur-romp SATURDAY NIGHT FEVE
LF-VALETDATION sheer sucker SKIMPLIFY worktails Z-LISTER arm restle ET
IGHT CONDESCENDANT flight dependent FRIGHT DECK gabbin pressure HO
blew JOHN THE LAPTIST lavawhory MATHZHEIMER's mile cry club ROAD A
AMTONITE touron TRAVELANCHE uso ADDVR bee break BLOCK-LISTED bl
PHONAL case DRAILING drimming E-MNESIA gpx HI-DEAF imonogamy IQU
APQUESTIONABLE mediacracy MISCALCULATE-COMERS mouse potato OVER
RVER phony call POST-MODEM textual frustration TIVOTE tone deaf YELLULA
-GORE-Y belting point BIODEBATABLE buyosphere CARBON DIOX-RIDE cole
SPAIR CONDITIONING fossil fools GREENHOUSE ASSES handy wipe HYBRIS
ortwear MILE HIGHGRAINE mitten kitten PIT-FALL priustoric RAINXIETY
OW FLAKE tendenitis WOOLLY BULLY brown nosed reindeer CRYDAY THE 13
idel robber EGGSNOG erin go bra-less HACK O' LANTERN hallmarketing HO
RLS jew-ish JINGLE BELLES little clown of bethlehem LITTLE WHITE LINE m
STLEHO mrs. claws PILL-GRIMS reigndeer games ROUND YON VIRGIN san
KY SEAMSTRESS/KINKY KNITTER thanks-mis-giving VIOLENT NIGHT, TRO

The
DAILY

CANDY
LEXICON

Words That Don't
Exist but Should

Virgin BOOKS

Distributed by Macmillan

Designed by Jason Snyder
Artwork by Sujean Rim

Library of Congress Cataloging-in-Publication Data

The DailyCandy lexicon : words that don't exist but should / by the
editors of DailyCandy. — 1st ed.
    p. cm.
 ISBN-13: 978-0-7535-1306-4
 ISBN-10: 0-7535-1306-4
 1. Vocabulary—Humor. 2. English language—Humor. I. DailyCandy.
com (Online resource)
 PN6231.W64D35 2008
 428.102'07—dc22
                              2008006078

To our readers

CNTENTS

NIGHTLIFE

TRAVEL

TECHNOLOGY

ENVIRONMENT

HOLIDAYS

ACKNOWLEDGMENTS

INTRODUCTION

I am an editor at DailyCandy. It feels funny to write that "I." As our faithful readers know, we prefer to shun the individuality of the first person singular for a collective voice. Why? The answer lies in the interconnectedness of our generation. (Well, that and our disturbingly codependent office dynamic.)

See, DailyCandy, the daily newsletter about fashion, food, and other trends, started in New York eight years ago. Since then it has grown to encompass twelve cities, ranging from the beaches of Miami to the rodeos of Dallas (okay, probably not rodeos). In each city, there's an editor. As we grew and more editors were hired, we noticed something interesting: No matter where the newbie was from, no matter what the difference in dialect, or the strangeness of the slang—the voice, the way of speaking, of communicating, rang familiar.

It's clipped. It's quick. It usually involves a bunch of parentheticals (in which you can hear the underlying, whispered wit). There are dashes galore because we're not even breathing between thoughts—just pausing. And, of course, some words *must* be stressed.

Where did it come from? How is it that women across the country and beyond, who had never even met, had a similar cadence to their voice that served as our very own secret handshake? How the hell should I know? I'm a trend expert, not a sociologist.

But if I had to guess, I'd say that sometime in our collective youth, the world became smaller as pop culture became bigger. Thirty years ago, if a woman from New York met a woman from Idaho, they'd have had limited cultural commonalities, having grown up on different food, entertainment, toys, even music. This is not to say there wouldn't have been similarities; they just wouldn't have been as vast as ours are today. When all our editors get together, if one person starts to hum the Chef Boyardee commercial that aired during *The Facts of Life*, we can all sing along. Chalk it up to cable TV (bless you, *Fraggle Rock*). In fact, our shared memories are so entrenched that Dany, DailyCandy's founder, has forbidden all stories that start with "Remember when you were in junior high . . ."

Speaking of, I remember when I was in college . . . a city girl dating a farmer (literally, his family had cows). When I was packing for my first trip to the country, I eschewed my new capri pants. I worried that the slightly odd-looking, cropped pants would be ridiculed in Small Town, America. When we pulled up to the barn, out came his sister, wearing the very same capri pants I'd left in my dorm room. By then, even farm towns had J. Crew—and Starbucks (she also liked soy milk, her cows be damned). This freedom from the limits of geography expanded the reach of cool.

DailyCandy didn't generate this wave, this obsession with pop culture ephemera, or this shorthand speak, but we rode it. And I can say, immodestly, that as that wave hit, as change in the way we communicate and the means by which we communicate crossed hairs, DailyCandy was there, putting this modern speak in print.

Years ago a young girl's life might hinge on whether or not she got a phone in her room for Christmas. Tweens talked for hours upon hours. Today's youth communicates almost exclusively in writing: IM, email, text, Facebook comments. It's like punctuation-less shorthand, the language of the future.

Communication has become increasingly non-spoken while the frequency of communication has multiplied tenfold (nonscientifically speaking). We "talk" constantly: be it an away message, an update on a message board, or a post on a blog, our movements are broadcast for all to read. ("In a meeting, then getting lunch, probably tuna fish.") As information has become easier to access, we've become quicker to share: more, more, now, now. It was this need for constant, fresh info that spawned DailyCandy. (We can tell our readers about a new designer bikini the moment the collection launches.)

And DailyCandy brought together a wonderful group of women who differ in everything: style, personality, sense of humor, ethnicity; but share a love of pop culture, and more importantly, language. We became part of this club, whose membership was deceptively large. And *that*—phew—is why our articles are anonymous. It's not editor Julie writing an article to a subscriber; it's one "club" member writing an email to another.

And this communication movement is cyclical; sometimes it returns to us. Case in point: A certain editor wrote an article about OhMiBod, a vibrator that connects to your iPod and vibrates to the beat of the music. At a party a few weeks later, a friend of a friend made a joke about DJing with an iRod. It was a reference to the title of the story, and an example of an insider passing on information, using "our" language.

Our love of words and all things new spawned our lexicons. First published in May of 2001, the DailyCandy lexicons are a dictionary of new words: words we've created, heard, or think we will hear soon. They're one of our oldest features and a rite of passage for each new editor. At first a daunting task, writing a lexicon quickly becomes a favorite. Unlike most of our other articles, they are collaborative. A theme is decided, an editor placed at the helm, and then the whole editorial team pitches in words.

Once your mind starts to work that way—honing in on new words—you start to hear them everywhere. Some start as offhand asides made by friends; others arise from need: what's it called when you date a man because he lives in your building? A "locationship." In the span of time it took to write this book, words that were innovative at the start became part of the mainstream by the end, e.g. "mouse potato" is now listed in the Oxford English Dictionary. Conversely, some words popped up too late to include in the manuscript, like these new favorites: "crymax" (to cry upon orgasm), "regaytionship" (an extremely close, same-sex friendship), and "nonversation" (to talk and say nothing).

Our fondness for turning a pun and playing with words shouldn't belie the power of those words. DailyCandy articles have a profound effect on their featured subjects. For example, the couple behind The Cookie Sandwich Co. were broke. They'd just had a baby. And their house was hit by the San Diego wildfires. Yeesh. DailyCandy to the rescue. After getting coverage in our national edition, the happy family woke up to hundreds and hundreds of orders. Plus, they got calls from celebrities, *Bon Appetit*, QVC, Costco, Williams Sonoma, *The Rachael Ray Show*, MSNBC, and more. Goodbye poor house, hello maid service.

Now, granted, not everyone reacts quite so positively (raise your hand if you remember the ill-received urinal story of 2004). But more often than not, we find that we affect change—the world has fewer lawyers and more jewelry makers, for one thing. Our power as tastemakers is due to the remarkable loyalty of our readers, the awesomeness of our subjects, and, of course, the power of words.

CHARACTERS

Some might call this a cast of characters; more truthfully, it's a cast of caricatures. The personalities who sit in DailyCandy's edit pen are too many and too messy to include, so we've merged them into seven—the deadly sinners if you will. Names may be changed, but the innocents at this office have been long lost.

Heidi

If fried catfish could talk, they'd tell you that Heidi had fried them with her eyes. Southern politesse coats a deep cynicism and hatred of most people, which in turn coats a heart of gold—much like a turducken of the human psyche. Heidi isn't mean, she's just honest, and usually the fools she doesn't suffer gladly aren't us, so we love her dearly. At arm's length, of course.

Simone

After a stint in L.A. auditioning for B-movies led to a too-close-for-comfort brush with Scientology, Simone returned East to hone her sarcasm and Seasonal Affective Disorder. Known for arriving at work still dressed in last night's clothes, Simone has a puppy named Puppy and considers *The Other Boleyn Girl* a manual for good living.

Delilah

Known for her quick wit and quicker temper, Delilah enjoys verbal jousting and tea time. She had an intern once, but lost her. Her motto is "I'm not crazy, I'm right"—Delilah believes that if people would only listen to her sound advice, instead of dismissing it as the ramblings of a madwoman, they'd be happier and a lot less stupid. Oh, and her favorite movie is *Apocalypse Now*.

Gwen

If you were to run a marathon at a respectable speed, swing by a rave to hear your DJ friend from Myanmar spin, and then pop into a scotch-drinking contest on the way home, you'd see Gwen everywhere you went, and then you'd see her at the office the next morning, looking cheery.

Lily

Fresh-faced, sweeter than Pixie Stix, and quicker than a licorice whip, Lily spent her childhood summers at Jesus Camp and now spends nights making out with Internet impresarios. Master of both humor and friendship, she relaxes to the tunes of Dolly Parton and Led Zeppelin. She's rumored to have inspired Tina Fey's character on *30 Rock*.

Boss

Simply put, he's the man. And we've lived with his boot on our necks for so long that we can't tell love from his tattered sole. He keeps us in line with a tender yet firm tyranny. He's cheaper than a half-off sale at the dollar store, more verbose than most politicians, and just as wily. Boss enjoys white-water rafting and watching videos of himself white-water rafting.

Tech Boys

For some reason they requested that they sit in a whole separate room last year. They've seen us try on bra samples in the middle of the office and they've heard more about our sex lives than our gynecologists, but they still pretend not to be scared of us. There are our foils, friends, and faithful flirtations. Look for their upcoming book: *Control, Alt, Delete: DailyCandy, Mind Control, and the Fragile Male Psyche*.

WORK

n. Employment. The daily grind. The only reason you wear anything other than pajamas. The ole ball and chain that you can't even sleep with.

Welcome to the DailyCandy office, located in beautiful downtown Manhattan. On your left, you'll find the edit staff; to the right, sales; and locked up in the back, the tech department (there are boys there!). What's that at your feet? Oh, it's the DailyCandy dog brigade: Puppy (Shih-tzu), Count Huckleberry (Boston terrier), Camille (pug), Oliver (French bulldog), and Moe (Yorkshire terrier). Wandering the office, making mischief, these critters are just as much our coworkers, if not more so, than their human counterparts.

Don't be fooled by the freewheeling atmosphere. As Mom used to say, it's called "work," not "fun." (Then again Mom also said that boys don't like loose women. And that's not true.) We know that sometimes your job can transform you into a tightly coiled ball of rage and someone needs to pay. And by "someone," you mean that bitch in finance who stole your miniature-horse-as-traveling-mailroom idea. Or maybe you, like we do, think that work is fun. What could be better than staring at a computer screen in a cage-sized space with poor lighting for nine hours a day? Nothing! (The Boss made us write that.)

Let's be honest, if a little sappy: The office is the place you spend most of your life, and working with the same people day after day, year after year, is the best chance most of us have to meet lifelong friends, mates, or tech guys with whom we really, really regret hooking up with after that ill-fated and immediately discontinued "Liquid Lunch" brainstorming series.

At work emerge not just friends of a particular kind, but words of a particular sort. Inventing ways to describe office quirks is a useful form of team bonding—especially when the budget for real team bonding was slashed last quarter. Our real-life friends may understand us, but our work friends sit with us through that health insurance presentation in which the head of HR describes his wife's chafed nipples. When you attempt to repeat this story to a colleague without

inducing the same gag reflex caused by the original event, you come up with euphemisms. These code words are used again and again, becoming classics. Here are a few of ours:

ACCOUNTING TERROR

n. The fear that you will be punished for your inappropriate work expenses. *(Suzie tried to expense a bikini wax. She's in total accounting terror.)*

AIM

acronym. To Actively Ignore Messages from annoying chat buddies while blaming the server for the lost connection.

Sometimes the editors who work from home want to IM about the gripping episode of *Oprah* they just watched. This always seems to happen when those of us in the office are actually feeling productive, so we AIM from them. They haven't seemed to catch on to the "server" lies.

APATHY HOUR

n. What happy hour usually feels like. *(If tonight's apathy hour is anything like last week's, Cathy will deliver Part II of her "why won't they promote me, I work so hard and no one gives me any credit" screed.)*

BAD RECEPTION-IST

n. The receptionist who never received the call that the '80s are over. She's also prone to hiding packages you're expecting from ShopBop.com and hanging up on the one desirable guy who's ever tried to track you down at work. (*What's with the bad reception-ist's* Working Girl *hair?*)

BLUETOOTHSOME

adj. Word describing someone so attractive that his/her hotness is not significantly diminished by the wearing of a bluetooth earpiece.

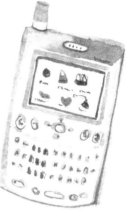

CEOVERKILL

n. 1. When your boss makes you write a lexicon. 2. When the boss gets you a book deal with said lexicons.

CONFERENCE CRAWL

n. The incredible physics-defying manner in which time slows down during a conference call. (*Oh gawd, if Tom's leading the conference crawl, we better bring a pillow. And some vodka. And a copy of* Harry Potter.)

DESK BURN

n. Injuries sustained during in-office sex. (*It's so obvious the bad reception-ist's limp is due to desk burn. Whore.*)

E-MAUL

v. To stalk someone via email.

GOLDEN PARATROOPER

n. Someone who is constantly failing upward and benefiting outrageously from his/her apparent failures. (*Dude, they just moved the golden paratrooper into that corner office with the giant mahogany desk and mini-fridge. When will they open their eyes and see what a freaking shammer she is?!*)

MEGO

acronym. My Eyes Glaze Over. The drugged-out sensation one gets when poring over spreadsheets or instruction manuals.

Delilah is always late handing in her expense reports. She blames it on her MEGO. Ethan, our accountant, doesn't believe it's a real physical ailment. Neither does the medical community.

MISSENGER

n. The inevitability that you're in the bathroom when a delivery arrives.

NO CC UMS

n. The pesky emails that everyone gets—whether they're relevant to the recipients or not.

Ah, the dreaded "reply all." There's someone (she knows who she is) who loves to share, emailing every single one of us, including those in London and Dallas, the vital stats of her lunch. (*Tepid. Cabbage-filled. Mildly spicy. Few drops of wayward duck sauce on the edge.*)

PHONE ZIT

n. The recurring chin zit that results from spending too much time on the phone.

PROMOTION SICKNESS

n. The queasy feeling one gets when someone really stupid gets promoted. (*Rob's such a kiss-up. His golden paratrooping gives me promotion sickness.*)

REPLY-ARRHEA

n. Email incontinence; an inability to stop emailing.

This is an unfortunately common affliction, especially among our joke-forwarding mothers who are just getting the hang of this "inter-web" thing.

SUPER CASUAL FRIDAY

True story.

n. When you come to work on Friday wearing the same thing you wore on Thursday (minus your cardigan and your watch, which you mysteriously left somewhere. After you send a messenger to pick them up, they arrive in a plastic bag sans note.).

TINE-GID-ISH?

expression. Very fast, slurred word designated for asking the question "What time is it?" when one is just too darn busy, or confused, to enunciate.

WISHFUL DRINKING

v. To drink excessively on a wintry night based on the desire for work to be canceled the next morning due to snow.

LOVE

n. Romance. Relationships. Sex. Lack of sex.
The emotion you hope will save you from dying
cold and alone in a room filled with cats.

We DailyCandy girls pride ourselves on defying stereotypes. Contrary to popular belief, the office is no *The Devil Wears Prada/Sex in the City* hybrid. (Some of us are wearing H&M and experiencing a dry spell.) But it might be fair to say that above the din—dogs barking, phones ringing, Delilah screaming—a certain topic might frequently arise: last night. So in a chapter focused on dating, sex, and everything in between (dry humping), you'd think the cup would runneth over.

You might ask if our experiences were too specific, too personal, too unique to merit their own words. I mean, does everyone need a name for a balding, unemployed, middle-aged man who leaves his darling longtime girlfriend for his twenty-year-old French intern? Because we do. And that name is Chris Oliver. (And he lives at 455 East 79th Street, apartment 2B. Send hate mail.)

But it turns out, no matter how bizarre, all our stories are relatable.

To wit: a certain DailyCandy editor set up a coworker with a gnome, who was 5'4" and still lived with his mother. And while that experience is Simone's cross to bear, alone, we have all experienced the brutal setup: a mother/cousin/friend who follows the disastrous he's-single-she's-single-they're-perfect-together formula (without taking into account that she's a vegan and he's a Republican). That meddler deserves to be named, so that when you return from the pit of blind date hell, you can smack her (gently) and tell her she's a "mental Yentl."

It turns out that no matter how specific (and horrific) our tales, when it comes to men, we've all been there, done him, and will probably do him again.

Here, some useful words for your romantic trials and titillations:

ALTARCATION

n. A heated, angry dispute between a couple regarding the details of their wedding. (*Honey, no, we did* not *discuss letting your Uncle Larry, a.k.a. "The Stuttering Wonder," do a reading.*)

AM-BUSHED

v. When your waxist takes off more than you had intended before the big date.

AMORAPHOBIA

n. Fear of love.

BLUE BALLSY

adj. The nerve of a man to claim that blue balls are scientific.

To the guy in O'Toole's who was wearing the backwards hat and Raider's jersey: We're not in high school anymore. We know it doesn't really hurt. We checked. On Wikipedia.

BOREPLAY

n. The worst kind of foreplay, which rarely, if ever, leads to intercourse.

CONDAMN

n. When your toilet gets clogged because you tried to flush a condom.

CUNNALINGUIST

n. A guy who's all talk and no action when it comes to going downtown.

DEBAUCHELOR

n. A groom whose bachelor party is particularly raunchy.

DIZO

acronym. Dual Income, Zero Orgasm. The all-too-typical, busy working couple.

FLACID

acronym. Failed Lovers Against Caller ID, inspired by that moment of weakness when you're Bridget Jones-ing to hear the jerk's voice one more time, so you fruitlessly call and hang up. Pathetic, yes. Possible, no, not since the invention of Caller ID.

Actually, in an incredibly unscientific poll conducted in the office, every single one of us denied calling a guy and hanging up. Yet another unscientific poll concluded that many of us are liars.

GHAG

acronym. Girl-HAting Girl. The one whose only friends are guys.

GUYATUS

n. A hiatus from guys. (*Thanks, but no thanks. I'm kind of on guyatus.*)

HEADHUNTER

n. A guy who is always on the search for a blowjob.

HOBEAU

n. A less-than-hygienic boyfriend.

INEBRIDATE

v. To regularly and repeatedly have drunken intercourse (never sober) with the same person. (*If my liver could take it, I'd inebridate John for at least another couple of months.*)

Gwen's handsome, clever, usually smart boyfriend has trouble understanding what constitutes cleanliness. He is not averse to showering, per se. It's just that once clean, he puts on the same pair of pants he's been wearing all week (while bike riding, deejaying smoky clubs, schlepping turntables on the filthy subway). The very same pair that were crumpled in a ball and thrown into the dirty laundry pile. Never once considering putting a pair of undies on underneath.

LADY BUSINESS CASUAL

adv. When your hoo-ha is past due for a wax. (*I'm rolling lady business casual this week, so I can't go home with anyone.*)

LOCATIONSHIP

n. A relationship based solely on proximity, such as with your neighbor.

MAID OF DISHONOR

n. The wedding attendant who alters her dress to show lots o' cleavage, then sleeps with the best man.

This phrase was coined after a certain editor attended a wedding and had a *very* good time. She claims that, one, she did not have the dress altered (her boobs are just that big). And two, the groom *told* her to be friendly to his out-of-town cousin.

MANBIGUOUS

adj. A quality in a man by which his behavior, sexual and otherwise, raises question about his sexual orientation. (*When Mike asked if her shoes were Louboutins while watching* Dancing With the Stars, *his gay status went from manbiguous to confirmed.*)

MASTURFAKER

n. A guy who claims he doesn't masturbate.

NUPTUALPALOOZA

n. A wedding weekend that's as action-packed as a three-ring circus.

PDR

acronym. Public Display of Rejection. When a couple fights in front of other people.

ROCKAFELLA

n. A groom who picks a ring for its size and ostentation. (*Sure, she's marrying for love. But it doesn't hurt that Joe's a rockafella.*)

SCOODGE

n. Sex that doesn't "count" because there was no completion due to technical difficulties. (*He was way too drunk . . . we just scoodged.*)

Some people might contest this word, claiming that there's no such thing as scoodge because the act is in the intent not the completion. To those people we respond, "I did NOT sleep with him, you dirty, filthy liar."

SCUM

acronym. Self-Centered Urban Male. The breed is fairly easy to spot. He usually wears a suit to work and only looks up from his BlackBerry when a scantily clad girl walks by.

SNOOPID

adj. To leave an obvious trail when snooping though your mate's belongings. (*She left his journal open on the bed. So snoopid.*)

VIR(TUAL)GIN

n. One who claims she's a virgin because she only has, um, alternative sex.

WHITE RUSSIAN ROULETTE

n. The final drink that sends you home with whomever you're talking to at the time. *(That last round of white Russian roulette almost had me going bareback with the barback.)*

WHOR D'OEUVRE

n. A girl who puts out before dinner.

FOOD

n. 1. That which fuels the body. 2. That which fuels the soul. 3. That which you projectile-vomited onto a date's lap. 4. That which causes certain people to miss the fact that you are a beautiful, intelligent person and not Crazy Vomit Girl. *Syn.* see "joy," "pain," "female neuroses (undifferentiated)"; *ant.* see "Velveeta," "Mountain Dew," "Spam."

At DailyCandy, it's our job to have opinions about food. At least, that's what we tell ourselves while stuffing our pie holes with, you know, pie. But as for everyone, food functions on many levels for us: nourishment, beloved friend, formidable foe, therapy topic, constant companion. (You put "candy" in your company's name and see if the Skittles don't start pouring in.) When we're not actually eating the stuff, we're writing about it, ordering it, or even arguing about it—we won't soon forget the Great Sandwich Debate of '07, in which Lily "Mayo Is the Devil's Condiment" Laurence narrowly defeated Heidi "Bring Out the Hellmann's" McCoy. Our editors have tracked trends from Scarsdale to South Beach, raw foods to sojutinis—and have even become foodie personalities in their own right. (Our L.A. editor has been known to bake straight through 'til morning.)

Of course there's the flip side to eating—namely, the not eating. We at DailyCandy have heard about this "dieting" and in response we've divided into two camps: the haves and the have not eaten carbs since 2002, the waste nots and the want not to consume calories, those who like to chew the fat and those who like to chew the fat then spit it out. Kidding, kidding. For a company full of women, we eat a shocking amount of donuts (whole wheat donuts).

Not surprisingly, we've memorialized many a culinary incident in the lexicon, from the time Delilah "Are You Gonna Finish That?" Brown (allegedly) absconded with Gwen "Who Moved My Cheese?" Carter's lunch, to the ongoing debates on various fads ("Small plates: an idea whose time has come, or just plain un-American?"). Because ultimately, it's DailyCandy's job not just to report on the food in our cities but to find words to convey the enthusiasm and passion it inspires in us (just ask Simone "A Celebrity Chef in Every Port" Benson). And in order to do that, we sometimes have to make them up.

FOOD

BRATKINS

n. Bad mood brought on by lack of sugar and carbohydrates in one's diet.

BRO YO

n. Yogurt intended to appeal to men, often in flavors like chocolate or cheesecake.

CARB BOMB

n. An assortment of fresh breads given out at a restaurant and continually replenished until the meal is served. *(Watch out, Ms. Atkins, it looks like that waitress is about to drop a carb bomb!)*

CARBONARA FOOTPRINT

n. Obvious and deleterious effects of overindulgence in creamy pasta dishes.

CEREAL MONOGAMY

n. A slavish devotion to one particular breakfast cereal. *(After three boxes of Cocoa Pebbles, I began to suspect he was a cereal monogamist.)*

CRAPPUCCINO

n. A poorly made coffee beverage that cost upwards of $4.

> After the Boss's email (reproaching us for leaving the office too many times during the day to fill our poor, energy-deprived bodies with legal speed, a.k.a. caffeine), a small, cracked-out lobbying group (spearheaded by the Tech Boys) was put in place to order a fancy, in-house coffeemaker. Turns out that the damn thing not only costs a fortune to refill, but it also creates a ton of superfluous waste. It's our personal crappucino machine.

CRAPAS

n. One of the many bad versions of the "small plates" craze. *(C'mon, bite-sized nachos are total crapas.)*

FOODILICIOUS

adj. A term describing really attractive food.

The winning foodstuff in Get Baked!, the first DailyCandy interoffice bake-off, was a batch of fried pretzels, which won solely because of their come-hither paper parchment sacks—complete with grosgrain ribbon trim and decadent dipping sauces. They weren't even a *baked* item, which should have been grounds for disqualification, says a completely not bitter loser, whose rustic granola cookies did not garner a single vote. Stupid judges.

FRUCT UP

adj. Containing large amounts of high-fructose corn syrup. *(Sure it's fat-free but it's fructed up.)*

GRUEL INTENTIONS

n. The determination to eat only healthy, bland food.

HAITRESS

n. Angry waitress. *See also:* haiter.

ICKYMAKI

n. A frightening sushi offering.
(That octopus looks like ickymaki.)

KITCHEN AID

n. A chef groupie.

MARSHMELLOW

adj. The food-induced crash and
coma following a sugar/dessert binge.

Upon starting her new job at DailyCandy, Lily was
warned of the freshman DailyCandy fifteen, gained
from the excitement of daily cupcake deliveries,
surprise cookie shipments, and various snacks brought
to the office for "research purposes." Mom isn't here to
tell you not to eat champagne truffles at 10:30 in the
morning. Or to warn you against eating the third slice
of Lombardi's pizza when it's on the company dime.

MARTYRINI ·············

n. A drink ordered after a particularly bad day.

MEAN CUISINE

n. Tiny portioned, disgusting tasting frozen food.

ORGANIC PANIC

n. The sudden need to shop at farmers markets/carry reusable shopping bags/ create a compost heap in your apartment.

In an effort to bring back the good old days of publishing houses (we weren't born then, but we saw it in the movies) we built a mini-bar in the edit pen. We are happy to report that Sugar Hole Spirits now operates daily, between the hours of 4 and 6 p.m.

Heidi was all burgers and fries until she moved to Brooklyn and joined the food co-op. Now she throws an eco-conscious fit at the sight of aspartame (a.k.a. poison powder).

PST

acronym. Poppy Seed in Teeth, pronounced "pssst" so as not to alert everyone else at the table.

RAWFUL

adj. Term describing really gross raw-food menu items. (*Did you guys taste the rawful "pizza crust" made from dehydrated carrots and brine-soaked cashews?*)

SALAD SPINSTER

n. A girl who sits at home eating healthy dishes for one. *See also:* boring.

SCHLOCKTAIL

n. Lame, themed drink, often seen at cheesy events and made with some sort of flavored liqueur. (*Keep that Raspberry Beret Bomb away from me. I don't drink schlocktails.*)

DailyCandy had a swank party last year to celebrate something or other. The reason none of us can remember exactly what we were celebrating is that despite our protests to the contrary, the Boss insisted on serving sugar-rimmed, fruity drinks, with cutesy names like Candy Cane and Daily Slammer. To avoid the sweet drinks, we staffers chose the only other available liquor: tequila. Toward the end, a certain employee attempted to sneak out with a prop candy jar stuffed in her purse.

SHARON VON MUNCHAUSEN

n. Friend who comes over and eats you out of house and home.

SINABLER

n. Someone who's a bad influence on your diet. *(Wanna split the fries?)*

SOY CAPITAN

n. Someone who substitutes soy for all normal foods. *See also:* seitan worshiper.

SPAMMELIER

n. 1. A sommelier who gives you too many choices. 2. Someone who's an expert on canned meats.

One of New York's health-conscious editors decided to try the Master Cleanse. For ten straight days, she was *supposed* to ingest nothing but a cocktail comprised of water, lemon, cayenne pepper, and maple syrup. The rest of us, in protest or perhaps spite, decided to eat more sumptuously than ever (pizza, disco fries, Haagen Dazs) right in front of her. The starving editor, pale and slumped in a corner, folded after two long days. Her first morsel: a bucket of day-old fried pickles.

TART FUEL

n. Girlie drinks, e.g., cosmos, kirs, or anything that tastes like Kool-Aid.

TASTY DE-LIE

n. The false belief that Tasti D-Lite is healthy.

TRIPE-IDATION

n. Fear of innards and other scary foods. *(That bone marrow gave me serious tripe-idation.)*

SHOPPING

n. The insatiable pursuit of materialistic fulfillment.
Relief for the burning sensation
caused by dollar bills in the wallet. The preferred
method for going into debt.

Picture this: a fashion closet brimming with designer clothes, bags, and shoes. At your disposal. All the time.

We hear these sanctuaries actually exist at some fashion pubs. Unfortunately, DailyCandy is not one of them. We do get a few perks, mainly in the form of cupcakes. (I guess it's the "Candy" name, but if people are going to send us any sample, they're usually of the sugary variety.) So unfortunately, the closest thing we have to a fashion closet is Delilah's mysterious "prop closet." She claimed the junky space when we moved into our office (no one protested). There's a rumor that it houses a shrine to Widespread Panic. But those who have caught a glimpse inside claim that there are wires hanging down from the ceiling, and that its contents include two slightly worn Cabbage Patch Kids and a collection of slap bracelets.

So, since we can't go pilfer some communal fashion paradise, we shop. A lot. Everywhere. Some of us are bargain hunters while others understand the importance of occasionally sacrificing good credit for a good outfit in the interest of retail therapy (it's cheaper than Xanax).

Some of us love nameless, underground boutiques while others have a sixth sense for flea markets and vintage. Gwen shops the top designers, and Lily, in turn, shops Gwen's closet. During work, we all find solace at the new Forever 21 that just opened up directly below our office (call it market research). And, of course, there are the sample sales that we write about as much for our readers as for ourselves.

Shopping, in many ways, is like sex: it's best to avoid it when drunk. It's fun to do online. And just checking out the goods (window shopping) without sealing the deal can be extremely unsatisfying.

To alleviate the frustration, some words you might buy:

ACHILLES HEEL

n. Your weakness for pretending to fit into the last pair of size-six boots when you're really an eight. *(She stumbled home in her new Loeffler Randalls thanks to her Achilles heel.)*

AMPLE SALE

n. A sale that consists of pieces in only ginormous sizes.

DISDRESS

n. The agony caused by having to strip in communal dressing rooms at sample sales.

On the contrary, if we had to think of a word for someone who reveled in nudity, her own nudity, it would be, um, Simone. Simone has no qualms disrobing centerstage to try on new clothes, and it's shocking that neither the Boss nor any of the Tech Boys have walked in on one of her in-office changes, although there's speculation she wouldn't flinch if they did.

DRESSAUSAGE

n. A girl who has squeezed herself into clothing that is way too small for her because she refuses to admit the article no longer fits.

Our Chicago editor was walking along Michigan Avenue when she saw her high-school boyfriend. After an awkward conversation about their current whereabouts (he thought DailyCandy was a porn site), she went to give him a business card, but it dropped. When she bent down to pick it up she heard a rip and realized her jeans had split, ass out. Playing it cool, she asked if he recognized the Jordache jeans she used to wear— he'd copped a feel while she was wearing them in high school.

DRESSING TOMB

n. The physics-defying, one-square-foot room in which you're expected to remove your pants. (*Stacy broke into such a claustrophobic sweat in the dressing tomb that she left without buying anything.*)

FABRIC-ATION

n. The involuntary impulse to lie when the salesgirl asks what size you are.

FEARRORS

n. Dreaded dressing-room mirrors that exacerbate every flaw on your body. (*After the fearrors made Leigh's thighs look like a topograhical map, she headed to the drugstore to buy skin-firming lotion.*)

FLEE MARKET

n. A flea market with questionable wares. *(Used mattresses? Underwear and tights out of their packaging? A bloody kitchen knife? Let's get out of this flee market ASAP.)*

Our Seattle editor loves to hit up the flea markets around Seattle, and she's known for having a radar for old, awesome records, antique furniture that would sell for thousands of dollars in New York, and vintage Jackie O-style dresses. A few weeks ago she bought a beautiful old trench coat. Now while she swears she usually washes stuff before she wears it, this time she went with instant gratification (masking the thrift smell with Jo Malone orange blossom). It wasn't until she got to the bar that she discovered the right-hand pocket was home to a condom wrapper. Gross.

GO GO GADGET ARM

n. The ability of shoppers to finagle and stretch their bodies around other shoppers/obstacles in order to snatch the last of a hot gadget or style.

INSHOPNIA

n. A disorder marked by making unnecessary online purchases in the wee hours due to insomnia.

MOOSE HOOF

n. The male equivalent of a camel toe, resulting from too-tight pants.

Spotting a moose hoof requires persistence and careful planning. We recommend visiting state fairs, gay clubs, and dude ranches out west (Gwen lived in Wyoming and fancies herself an expert on this particular fauna). Remember to have your cameras ready and stay quiet. If they spot you, they could attack.

MOUSE TRAP

n. An Internet purchase that looks a lot different upon arrival than it did in the picture.

REFLECTION PERIOD

n. The time spent contemplating whether you're being tricked by skinny mirrors and soft filter lighting.

RIPTAG

n. A last-minute purchase that you wear out of the store.

OUTLET MAUL

n. 1. When one buys a big designer's ugly garment because it's significantly on sale at an outlet mall. *(Who comes out on top after an outlet maul? Thrift stores.)* 2. To go to an outlet mall around the holidays.

PHARMASECRECY

n. The secret prescriptions you order overseas.

Hey, clothing isn't the only thing we buy.

During Lily's love affair with eBay, she purchased a long, flowy dress. When it arrived, she discovered the "dress" was actually a jumper with huge palazzo style legs. Careful examination of the seller's history (and the fact she called herself "iGotYouBabe") has Lily believing she bought a pair of Cher's pants.

SANDBAG

n. A women's unbelievably large "purse" that may or may not be holding cinder blocks (chiropractors are the real winners here).

Gwen has a gorgeous Miu Miu bag that she calls "the one big expenditure of my life." It goes with everything, which is good because it cost more than her rent and she might have to live in it one day. It's the size of a small city. On any given day, the contents may include: a mini pharmacy, her cat, Hobson, two airplane-sized bottles of Tanquerey, an iPhone, a rhyming dictionary, the first season of *Battlestar Galactica* on DVD, one fake mustache, and a roast beef sandwich sans bread.

SKEW-TIQUE

n. Stores that distort their clothes' sizes (can be either flattering or humiliating, depending on the direction in which they skew).

SHOPPINGS

n. The product amassed from a day out at the shops. (*"Babette, look at my shoppings!" she said in her thick New Jersey accent.*)

UN-MODEST MOUSE

n. A naggy salesperson who pulls the curtain back while you're changing.

VIVIAN RE-WARD

n. The feeling one gets after making a purchase just to snub a snobby sales associate. Named for the Julia Roberts character in *Pretty Woman*. (*Camille felt the Vivian Re-Ward as she walked out of the store, bags in hand, and said, "I may be young, but my credit card is grown up."*)

We love small boutiques, but sometimes their dressing rooms are nothing more than flimsy, linen curtains. One fine day, Heidi was trying on a bathing suit when an employee peeked through the curtain, unsummoned, to see if she needed anything. A mostly naked and completely furious Heidi told the salesperson precisely what she needed: "Can you get me a bikini wax? As you can see, I need one. Thanks."

WWKD

acronym. What Would Kate Do? The question to ask when determining if a particular outfit meets the fashion commandments. (*That frock's a sin. Miss Moss wouldn't be caught dead in it.*)

It's important to note that we use WWKD only when talking about fashion. We try not to ask ourselves WWKD when presented with illegal substances or drug-addled rock stars. (Though sometimes we might indulge just a little. Rock stars are hard to resist.)

NIGHTLIFE

n. Social activities, entertainment, and diversions pursued during the evening hours including but not limited to: drinking at bars, dining out, dancing at clubs, attending the theater, dumpster diving, watching movies, and experiencing non-sexual group physical intimacy at cuddle parties.

Here at DailyCandy we encourage a healthy dose of nighttime fun. And we appreciate and respect each person's decision on how to pass the evening hours—be it a quiet night at home on the couch, or a wild night at home on the couch. Of course, that doesn't mean we won't make fun of the Boss and his Second Life avatar the morning after.

But by and large, nightlife is a collective term that truly holds relative meaning to each one of us. Cinderella may have a midnight curfew, but we certainly don't. (Which is why you can sometimes find us napping on the floor of the tech office.)

We spend an awful lot of time together. Over the years our extracurriculars have encompassed the fairly tame (movies! popcorn!) to the physically taxing (there is no crying in DailyCandy dodge ball!) to the risqué (we don't call him "Handsy" for nothing). And there are certain universal truths when we all hang out together: Where there is wine, cheese follows. Where there is karaoke there is Delilah singing Bon Jovi. Lily and

Gwen, when left to their own devices, will end up in costume. Heidi will always be the first to leave the party (to hang out with her *real* friends). And someone— ahem, Simone—will inevitably use the "stepping out for fresh air" excuse to jump into a taxi.

In the end we can admit that the debilitating pub crawls, scene-y dinners, crappy one-night stands, 2 a.m. Korean spa appointments with strangers, and walks of shame to the office are all pursued in the name of good storytelling (Simone calls it journalism), but mostly as justification for ordering the hangover deluxe (burger and fries) at Buffa's Diner the next day.

So before donning your cloak of crazy and heading into the night, equip yourself with a few aspirin (preemptive) and a new vocabulary. Remember, ladies, it's eighteen to party, twenty-one to drink. Guys pay cover at the door.

AMATEUR NIGHT OWL

n. The guy/girl who parties hard all night long on Friday—only to spend the rest of the weekend recovering in bed.

COLLATERAL

n. A person you end up driving around all night with whom you didn't even want to hang out in the first place. (*I'd love to join you, but I don't think my collateral is on the list.*)

DANCE DANCE EVOLUTION

n. The fantastical notion, after a few rounds of drinks, that you are an incredibly gifted dancer.

Let it be known that The Wheelchair, The Lonely Crutch, The Sinking Canoe, and Wounded Knee are all moves conceived by various colleagues in various states of inebriation. Notice (also) that, when choreographed together, these moves resemble a troop of wounded soldiers. Led by Colonel Gwen and Deputy Lily, who fought to the death at the Battle of Slow Gin Alley. May those moves rest in peace.

DRESSED TO SPILL

adj. Used to describe a woman's precarious and flirtatious state of dress, wherein a great deal more than cleavage will likely be revealed. (*Look at Julia's nonexistent top. That girl is dressed to spill tonight!*)

FLEETING

v. Scheduling "a very important appointment first thing in the morning" in an attempt to hide from the office after a night of regretfully embarrassing moments.

Here's a lesson. If you are ever out at a work-related cocktail party with your colleagues and boss, and everyone cuts loose and gets rowdy and has a great time (pictures on a gossip blog the next day prove it), and everyone makes it to work the next day with a hangover *except* for your boss, and then the company gets a mass email from said boss saying something like *"am at meetings. They are about to cut my Internet access for the rest of day, but will have cell and BB,"* you can pretty much be sure that he's too hungover to face an office full of girls making fun of his dance dance evolution. Sorry, Boss.

FRIDEA

n. The belief that greasy onion rings, quesadillas, fried pickles, and bacon, egg, and cheese sandwiches make sensible bedtime snacks.

There are many good nights that end with bad ideas (that includes you, Snaggletoothed Guy). But there are many bad nights that end with the best ideas—which we will call disco fries. For some reason, it often takes consuming large quantities of liquor to come up with a genius plan like shoveling 4,000 calories into your gullet immediately before bed. Case in point: One night *after* Gwen unofficially broke the world record in vodka-tonic drinking (the same night she performed a contemporary interpretive dance to Prince's "Darling Nikki"), but *before* making it home, she not only had the smart idea to mop up her liver with a small paper pouch of French fried potatoes, but—after taking a spill on the sidewalk with said fries beneath her—she then had the foresight to go back and super-size the order in case there were any further missteps along the way.

INTOXICANTILEVER

n. The *one* responsible person in the group who offsets drunken behavior by holding back hair, driving sober, and remembering to close out the credit card tab at the bar.

LUSH FLUSH

n. The rosy hue one gets in her cheeks after a few too many glasses of wine.

MARGARITER

v. To serve someone a margarita for the express purpose of loosening her up. *alt.* margaritim. (*He's just sitting in the corner, Madeleine. If you're interested you're going to have to margaritim.*)

NONTOURAGE

n. A group of undesirable sycophants. (*The party was fun until Justin showed up with his nontourage.*)

PALET

n. A valet who takes especially good care of your car. (*Aw, you parked it right in front. What a palet.*)

PHOHOGRAPHER

n. The camera-wielding girl on the dance floor who takes hundreds of shots while using a seizure-inducing flash.

We asked some ex-interns, a.k.a. experts on all matters of Facebook self portraiture, about the state of the personal bio page on various social networking sites. They explained that there are over-exposed, narcissistic, camera-happy people, whose number of point-n-shoot pictures (of themselves) averaged somewhere in the hundreds. To be fair, the Tech Boys are dashing.

PTPD

acronym. Post-Traumatic Press Disorder. The freak-out experienced after being cited in Page Six or on an equally annoying gossip blog. *(To help cope with her PTPD, she threw her BlackBerry in the toilet and canceled her Internet connection for the month.)*

PUI

acronym. Planning Under the Influence. Plan-making late in the evening, especially with friends, for next-day activities, such as two-touch football, shopping, and brunch. These plans rarely, if ever, come to fruition.

REHOUNDING

v. To spring back from a nasty breakup by going to a bar, imbibing too much, making out with multiple, random sub-standard minors, and then throwing up in a corner.

RESTAUR-ROMP

n. A date that gets out of hand at a dinner table and/or bar area. *(After two bottles of wine my date turned into a full-on restaur-romp.)*

SATURDAY NIGHT FEVER

n. Often followed by a real fever, the delirium that comes over some women as they get (un)dressed for a Saturday night on the town, believing that the temperature is as much as twenty degrees warmer than it actually is. *See also:* skimplify.

SKY-BARRED

n. The condition of being excluded from evening planning for having suggested the Sunset Boulevard staple one too many times. (*You're sky-barred, sister. We'll let you know where we're going when we decide.*)

SELF-VALETDATION

n. Every now and then, when one parks on one's own, just to get away from it all.

SHEER SUCKER

n. A man (usually the kind who works in finance) who spends thousands of dollars on VIP memberships to tragically hip clubs where he buys $300 bottles of vodka for a group of people who will never remember his name.

SKIMPLIFY

v. To reduce the amount of cloth used to cover the body. (*TGIF—time to skimplify the wardrobe.*)

We've all hung out with this guy, once.

NAME: Mr. Moneybags

OCCUPATION: Ladies' Man

HEIGHT: Comparable to Napoleon

WEIGHT: In gold?

HOBBIES: Traveling, tanning, partying, using cash as kindling for camp fires, not committing, rubbing Rogaine on receding hairline

LAST SEEN: At all the right places

FRIENDS WITH: Fellow d-bag friends from prep school/ frat/b-school/trading desk, chicks I bagged/dumped/still want in my life so I can get to their friends/sisters

24-HR DAMAGE: More than your monthly salary

MOTTO: "Deny, deny, deny"

WORKTAILS

n. 1. Obligatory after-work drinks with clients.

2. An excuse for using the company credit card.

Z-LISTER

n. The dinner-party guest who bores you to sleep. (*That Z-lister over there won't stop talking about Sundance.*)

TRAVEL

v. To move from one place to another, even if the first
place is your bed and the second place is your couch.
To pack an inordinate amount of clothing and hop on
a plane, secure in the knowledge that you'll have the
appropriate attire if someone you haven't met yet just
happens to invite you to a costume party on a yacht or
if there's an avalanche in Bali.

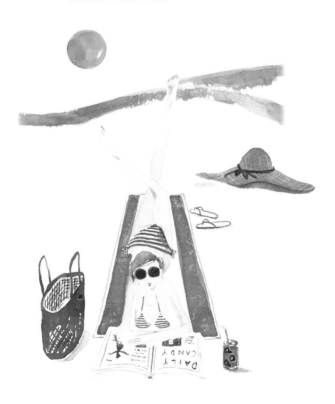

Pop culture is awash in travel references—and there's a reason. Life really is about the journey, and we spend many of our waking hours coming and going. Consider it: Sailing takes you away to where you're going. Big ole jet airliner carries you too far from home. You're leaving on a jet plane. You're going off the rails on a crazy train. However you're getting there, you've got miles to go before you sleep. And so do we, especially when the Boss tricks us into attending a weekend conference in Detroit during a baggage handler strike. (Never mind the connection through Indianapolis that saved him $17 per ticket.) Hitchhiking never seemed more appealing. (Kidding, kidding—that's illegal!)

Point is, for business or pleasure, travel is a big part of our lives. And it is at once a great joy and a giant headache. We've had our fair share of both, though it seems like the latter happens more often on work trips than fun trips. Which is totally fine, because who in her right mind wouldn't want to get stuck in Key West with a sexy French truffle salesman? (Actually, in hindsight, that trip to Florida was kind of a mistake. She would have been better off had she been not just delayed but rerouted to Kabul—but that's a tale for another time.)

Everybody gets stuck in a seat beside the bathroom or Chatty Cathy once in awhile. Everyone, at one time or another, has a suitcase full of sex toys flagged by security for careful, painstaking hand inspection. The phrase "We'll look back and laugh about this" is much more realistic when you have funny ways to describe the travails of travel. Here are some that have helped us through long customs lines and death-defying Central American cab rides.

ARM RESTLE

n. The ongoing battle waged with your seatmate over the middle armrest. Maneuvers include ELBOGARTING (slow advance of the elbow to gain ground) and RECLINE AND CONQUER (capturing the armrest during feigned or actual sleep).

ETA

acronym. Eons 'Til Arrival. Most often heard at the airport in San Juan, Puerto Rico. Used by gate agents who know darn well your flight is going to be canceled but make you wait six hours until they tell you.

A certain editor's flight was delayed on her way back to New York. She thought she'd kill the time at the airport Chili's. Loosened up by Bloody Marys, she got chatty with Mr. Business Trip on the stool next door. The next thing she knew, they were sharing jalapeño poppers, stories from their childhood, and hotel room information. Needless to say, she didn't mind that her plane home was canceled.

EXIT ROW

n. The no-holds-barred, angry fight at the podium to try to convince the agent one deserves to be switched to a seat in the exit row.

FLIGHT CONDESCENDANT

n. The flight attendant-cum-prima donna who rolls her eyes then glares at you with a death stare if you dare ask her for a pillow. Often seen gossiping at top volume with colleagues instead of conducting safety preparations for take-off.

FLIGHT DEPENDENT

n. Neighboring passenger who, flying solo, turns to you in search of company/a drinking partner/a date.

To avoid tempting flight dependents to engage, we suggest making a very visible show of taking Ambien, Klonopin, and/or Tylenol, then covering your entire head with a blanket. Pretty effective. (That's a joke. Take prescription medicine only as directed by your physician, Dr. Strangelove.)

FRIGHT DECK

n. The place from which the confident-sounding captain makes those terrifying announcements (*Uh, ladies and gentleman, from the fright deck this is Captain Hindenberg, and we have reached our cruising altitude of 36,000 feet. But I'm going to go ahead and keep the seatbelt sign illuminated, as we're going to hit some incredibly dangerous turbulence that may splinter the cabin and shoot you all off of this mortal coil once and for all. We'll check back in with you on the other side . . . in the meantime, sit back, relax, and enjoy the flight!*)

GABBIN PRESSURE

n. Sense of obligation to chat to the passenger next to you during a flight. (*Sorry I'm a little quiet and out of it, I'm just recovering from gabbin pressure—I sat next to a real flight dependent.*)

GIRLS

HOLY CRAP

n. The first visit to indoor plumbing after a weekend in the woods.

BOYS

JET BLEW

v.. When you fly across the country on a plane in which forty-one of the forty-two DirecTV channels do not work. (America's Next Top Model *premiere? Uh, no, I missed it . . . I flew jet blew.*)

JOHN THE LAPTIST

n. The guy in front of you who reclines his seat until his head is in your lap.

LAVAWHORY

adj. Describes a person, male or female, who thinks nothing of spending a good twenty-five minutes in one of the two economy-class lavatories available to two hundred people. They have the audacity to stay in there tweezing, reading, shooting heroin, you know, all while you hop around cross-legged outside.

MATHZHEIMER'S

n. The inability to calculate a foreign exchange rate without elaborate financial and/or tech support.

MILE CRY CLUB

n. The babies and children on a plane who spend the entire flight crying, screaming, and kicking your seat.

ROAD ASS

n. The delicious treat with whom you hook up when you're away from home.

You might meet road ass at a hotel bar (your totally hot bartender), at a chic restaurant (your totally hot waiter), or a swanky hotel (your totally hot bellboy). Those in the office who travel for business deny any knowledge of road ass, but if they're telling the truth, how'd we all know this word, huh?

On a flight from New York to San Fran, Heidi had three kids in front of her and three behind—all part of the same family—who yelled over her head, back and forth for five torturous hours. Their parents had chosen the hands-off approach—sitting their lazy asses in first class and coming by to "check up" but twice. On the way off the plane, Heidi witnessed the family's regrouping and calmly said to the father: "Too bad your guys are swimmers."

SCARY-ON

n. An oversize, overstuffed carry-on bag that should have been checked but instead jams up an entire overhead bin.

Delilah admits she is secretly happy when the jerks that bring scary-ons are forced to gate check.

SHAMTONITE

n. Summer house freeloader. *(Chad is such a Shamtonite. He's been hanging out in Bridgehampton for the past three weekends and he doesn't even rent.)*

A Shamtonite who had crashed at Lily's share house all summer and took twenty-minute showers twice a day actually had the nerve to ask her out when he coincidentally visited the office the following autumn as a salesperson.

TOURON

n. Tourist + moron. *(Don't even bother with the Louvre on a Saturday. It's overrun with tourons.)*

It's also impossible to walk down Broadway in front of the DailyCandy offices on pretty much any day of the summer, as tourons stroll four-deep on their way to the Old Navy that's so very different from the one back in Touronville.

TRAVELANCHE

n. The state of affairs when one little thing goes wrong and then everything snowballs toward disaster.

The city editors all come to New York twice a year for the summit—an all-expense paid trip to the greatest city of them all: New York. Boy, were they excited. Upon arrival at the NYC office, they were loaded on a bus and herded to the exciting state next door: New Jersey. That's right, someone had the brilliant idea to rent a party bus and go to Six Flags, Great Adventure. Which would have been great, if we were fourteen and at sleepaway camp. Instead, the Dallas editor got sick on the old wooden coaster. The London editor got sick on funnel cake. And the Philly editor got sick on the bus. The whole mess is now referred to as the Not-So-Great-Adventure, or the Great Travelanche of Aught-Six.

USO

acronym. Unidentified Stained Object. Hotel carpet or bedding that has mysterious marks. *(Alexis refuses to stay at subpar hotels due to her intense fear of USOs.)*

TECHNOLOGY

n. Gadgets and gizmos. Stuff with wires. Stuff
that's wireless. Machines that play music, email,
talk, and photograph. Any tool that enables you
to communicate without actually having to
talk to another person.

Some people—like our moms—think we must be technology experts since we work "in the Internet." Others doubt our computer savvy, like the Tech Boys, who, from the four-walled confines of the tech office, often hear us whining (okay, screaming) when our computers don't do what we tell them. (Turns out, yelling, "No, no, don't crash! Please, not now!" has absolutely no effect on your computer's processing skills.) To add insult to embarrassment, once one of the darling Tech Boys arrives on our side of the divide to mend the glitch, they simply click return and fix the problem, leaving us to marvel dumbly in their wake, "I swear it wasn't working a second ago."

But there is some tech knowledge in which we do take pride, namely anything in the field of non-verbal communication. When it comes to email, text, or IM, we are kings. The edit side of the DailyCandy office is jam-packed, yet none of us speaks (at least, not to each other. There is, on the other hand, plenty of talking loudly to one's mother about your wedding plans, Delilah). Do we not talk because we're a bunch of antisocial bitches? Yes. No! It's just because we all communicate via IM.

Everything that occurs in the DC office is underscored by a soundtrack of clickity-clack-clack-clack. It accompanies all happenings. Want to know how big of a splash your outfit or outburst had in the pitch meeting? Just listen to the rhythm of the keyboards. Watch as giggles pass from desk to desk like wildfire, the delay only the time it takes for Simone to key in, "OMG, Delilah is totally PO'd over the new desks that the Boss ordered from Ikea." Like a postmodern game of telephone, these little megabytes of sound bites shoot from the office to the city editors to the blogs, until eventually it becomes, "OMG, Delilah totally peed all over the new desks and it was the Boss's idea."

Technology moves at an ever-increasing speed; language, not so fast. DailyCandy bridges the gap with a smattering of words:

ADDVR

acronym. Attention Deficit DVR. The short-attention span garnered from fast forwarding though boring parts of TV shows.

BEE BREAK

n. The act of sneaking off to the bathroom in the middle of dinner to scroll through one's BlackBerry.

BLOCK-LISTED

adj. Permanently banned from all modes of virtual communication.

Since all the DCers communicate via IM, our screennames are live, online, all day (or should be). So if you happen to be young and single, you might accidentally drop your screen name to a new suitor, in case of emergencies. But when he turns out to suck, big time, you can't have him dropping "Hi's" while you're trying to work, so you block him. Eventually, you might have a whole blocked list ('cause you get around). One day, you might have to just change your IM name altogether, from cutie4life to SimoneisWorking.

BLUETOOTH FAIRY

n. The magical fairy that must live within your Bluetooth devices to enable them to communicate with each other. *(Little Bluetooth fairy of the cell phone, please tell the computer to email Bob.)*

BIPHONAL

adj. Able to hold multiple phones to your ears or in front of you at the same time, i.e., talking on your cell while texting on your BlackBerry.

CASE

v. To use the jarring style of ALL CAPITAL LETTERS in an email. Also known as virtual shouting. *(Dude, quit casing me!)*

DRAILING

n. Drunk emailing.

DRIMMING

n. Drunk instant-messaging.

E-MNESIA

n. The condition of having sent or received an email and having no recollection of it whatsoever.

GPX

n. A tracking system devised to monitor your ex's every move. (*Nancy uses MySpace as GPX.*)

HI-DEAF

n. The super sonic sound system that renders you temporarily hearing-impaired.

IMONOGAMY

n 1. The practice of chatting into only one window at a time. 2. When one relies solely on IM as a method of communication.

Of course, none of us have ever looked up an ex on MySpace, nor have we looked up his new girlfriend and then asked everyone in the office who was prettier.

As a result of our constant presence online (and lack of presence offline), many of our parents have started to ping us on instant messenger, happy to have a new way to bother (we mean talk) to us. However, the older generation hasn't quite mastered the IM. Consider the following from Lily's dad:

PapadontPreach: Dear Lily, Hi! How are you? Mom and I went for dinner with Aunt Suzie and Uncle Bob at the new Chinese place that opened on the corner of Second Street, right by where the old drycleaner used to be. We miss you. Love, Dad

IQUE

n. Your level of iPod expertise or lack thereof (*She doesn't have the nano? Must have a low iQue.*)

LAPTOPLESS

adj. Working on one's home computer while semi-clothed.

During the NYC transit strike, those of us who lived far from the office worked from home. (Those of us who lived close lamented we didn't live farther.) The Boss sent out a notice informing the staff that despite working from home, we were all expected to conduct ourselves as though it was a normal work day. Heidi responded to all: "The Brooklyn branch wears no pants!" "No pants Brooklyn" has since become a DC battle cry.

MAPQUESTIONABLE

adj. Word describing directions provided by MapQuest that somehow cause you to drive in an enormous figure eight.

MEDIACRACY

n. 1. The news you read online. 2. The celebrity coverage that is now considered news.

MISCALCULATE-COMERS

n. People who blame their tardiness on an inefficient GPS system.

MOUSE POTATO

n. The wired generation's answer to the couch potato.

OVERSHARED SERVER

n. A person who consistently hits "Reply All" when he/she should hit "Reply."

PHONY CALL

n. The call you make when you *pray* you'll get someone's voicemail. *(I'll phony call in sick when the boss lady's in a meeting.)*

POST-MODEM

n. The freak out you experience when your Internet goes dead.

TEXTUAL FRUSTRATION

n. A late-night text exchange that fails to result in old-fashioned lip-locking.

TIVOTE

n. The ballot you cast with your roommates as to which show deserves to be recorded. *(They TiVoted against my* Project Runway *proposition.)*

A certain editor once texted Gwen, "hey baby, wanna play doctor?" at three in the morning. Said drunken editor then explained that the text was intended for her late-night paramour, Paul, the podiatrist.

The edit staff often has online brainstorming sessions. For example, someone might want ideas for unconventional food predilections or songs with body parts in the title. On one such email thread, the subject turned to merkins (weaves for the hair—down there). Emails flowed back and forth, pictures followed. It wasn't until later that we realized the Boss had been included on the original email, and every one thereafter. Oops.

TONE DEAF

adj. Hearing your distinct ring tone even
when no one is calling. (*Is that my cell? Nope,
it's the elevator music.*)

YELLULAR

n. The loudness one adopts in response to a bad
cell-phone connection, in the misguided hope that
talking louder will improve it. (*I'm so embarrassed. I
went totally yellular at a restaurant last night.*)

ENVIRONMENT

n. Mother Earth. The biosphere. The not-always-so-great outdoors. The weather, without which your father would be at a complete loss for phone conversation material.

The DailyCandy office isn't exactly teeming with nature girls, with a few notable exceptions (okay, just one—Lily, who once let her boyfriend take her camping. Hilarity and whining ensued). Take for example, last year's company retreat, which took place at a resort known for its hiking, horseback riding, and rock-climbing. Two of the girls packed sneakers; the rest, a stylish assortment of wedges, sling backs, and flip-flops.

But even if you, like we do, err on the side of city mouse, the environment—and its increasingly dramatic mood swings—is undoubtedly a major player in your life. Maybe you're waging your own private battle with the weather gods (by wearing ballet flats in the dead of winter) or a more public one with your HR director (by dressing like a three-dollar hooker during the dog days of summer). Perhaps you're as spoiled as our Miami editor (who always keeps a bikini in her trunk, just in case), or maybe you're as whiny and miserable as our Seattle editor in February. (Note: Not possible.)

But no matter where you are or what the time of year, the air out there affects so much. A dark, stormy weekend means you can plant your butt on the couch and watch forty-eight straight hours of *Arrested Development*—guilt-free—the weather a myth on the other side of your drawn shades.

And while we've always known that Earth Day should be every day, we're more aware of our impact on the environment by the minute. After all, who wouldn't pay attention to Mr. DiCaprio? Point is: We're quite serious about going easier on the planet. (Well, maybe not Simone. She admitted to nodding off midway through *An Inconvenient Truth*.)

Of course, the environment is a pressing topic. But that's not to say it's the most scintillating of conversation starters. After all, how many times can you chitchat with your lonely upstairs neighbor about the weather? Nineteen. Every single time you turn down his invitation to grab a drink by mumbling, "Sure is cold out. Bye." And how many ways are there to remind your boyfriend that glass bottles do not go in the aluminum recycle bin? Two. One: silently re-sort the recyclables while shooting him the stink eye. Or two: withhold sex.

Thus, to spice things up in the fresh air department, we've developed our own environmentally conscious vocabulary over the years—meant to sum up and poke fun at our natural habitat.

AC/DC
n. Air Conditioning Debate Club, the battle between the yea's (blast it) and the nay's (crack a window).

In a roomful of women, someone (Heidi) is always cold. So all summer long, the AC is flipped on and off, then on, then off, then on, with increasing ferocity. Team Hot sits stewing and sweating in skimpy sundresses, while Team Cold is bundled up like it's the Ice Age.

AL-LE-GORE-Y

n. He who represents the "abstract" idea of global warming and everything that comes with it. (*My little sis, the recycling Nazi, is so Al-le-Gore-y.*)

BELTING POINT

n. The space under your parka where your waist would be if you hadn't spent all fall bulking up for hibernation.

BIODEBATABLE

n. 1. The questionable products that claim to be green. 2. Something that shouldn't be worn just because it's green. *(I don't care if those biodebatable jeans are organic, they're fugly.)*

We once got a face mask sample that was green (as in eco-friendly, not Kermit-colored). It was called Recyclable Faces. We should have been leery. But ever the pioneers, we tried it. The next morning, half of us were covered in hives. It turns out not everything should be made from corn meal and dung.

BUYOSPHERE

Recyclable Faces retails for thirty bucks.

n. The mental space in which you happily pay extra for green, organic, or eco-friendly products without blinking an eye. *(My dry cleaner has entered the buyosphere, with $20 filtered-water hand washes.)*

CARBON DIOX-RIDE

v. What the greenhouse asses (see below) took you on when lying to you about the effects of global warming.

COLD FRONTIN'

v. The act of baring cleavage, no matter how cold it gets, to look hot at the bar. *(Stacy's nips betray how her cold frontin' is affecting her.)*

DESPAIR CONDITIONING

n. An unexpected waft of cool air (e.g., from a passing bus) that is at once disgusting and welcome in ninety-degree heat.

FOSSIL FOOLS

n. People who don't realize the negative impact of their actions. *(Jamie packed her groceries in a reusable tote and then loaded them into her Hummer.)*

Our L.A. editor, was invited to a totally green wedding. The invitations were printed on recycled paper. The dress was made from organic fabric. All the food was sourced from local farmers. Even the utensils were made from corn husks. And the gifts were donated to Save the South Floridian Pygmy Population. The location of the wedding: the Maldives. It was after her ten-hour, oil-depleting, fuel-wasting, gas-guzzling flight that she coined the phrase "fossil fool."

ENVIRONMENT

GREENHOUSE ASSES

n. The silly people who led you to believe that the environment was a-okay. (*I was in denial for years, all because of those greenhouse asses.*)

HANDY WIPE

v. When you've used the last tissue and have nothing left but your hand. (*Cindy, hand me a tissue. I don't want to handy wipe before the managers' meeting.*)

HYBRIS

n. Excessive pride based solely on one's hybrid car.

LAST RESORTWEAR

n. Old, tattered, or unfashionable clothing worn simply because it's too cold to care. (*Do you think that guy didn't ask Susan out because he saw her in last resortwear?*)

MILE HIGHGRAINE

n. The splitting headache caused by camping (usually due to a combination of altitude, an air mattress, and heavy drinking around the campfire).

MITTEN KITTEN

n. The evil fairy who steals one mitten or glove from your coat pocket every winter.

PIT-FALL

n. 1. The unavoidable underarm stains one gets from wearing tight, nonbreathable tees in ninety-degree weather. 2. One's inability to avoid wearing tight, nonbreathable tees in ninety-degree weather.

As stated in AC/DC, the body temps (and hormone levels) here at DailyCandy run rampant. So while most people wear junky jackets and oversized snow boots outside and strip down to slinky shoes and lightweight shirts at work, not so at DailyCandy. Since someone is always cold, the office has a stash of ratty Champion sweatshirts and slankets (giant hooded blankets that give the wearer the grim reaper look). It's also not unusual for someone to walk around in Snoopy slippers.

PRIUSTORIC

adj. From a time long ago, before hybrids.

RAINXIETY

n. Stress associated with driving in even the lightest drizzle. *(Dude, get over your rainxiety already. It's not like it's snowing.)*

SKNOWMAN

n. The ski bum who knows way too much about winter sports. *(Sorry I'm late, my sknowman decided to teach me to board and my butt's still frozen.)*

Gwen's boyfriend attempted to take her on a ski weekend. When she got back, we all asked how she did. She reported that it was a complete success. She excelled in all areas: lounge napping, fireplace relaxing, hot-tub soaking, and cocoa drinking.

SNOW FLAKE

n. A person who cancels plans at the slightest mention of precipitation.

Simone is known for her famous last words, "See you there." The following day, when called out on being a no-show, she's been known to cite the weather: It was too cold. Or too hot or too cloudy. Or just too sunny. Lame.

TENDENITIS

n. A disorder suffered by those who tend to wear ridiculous heels on icy sidewalks.

WOOLLY BULLY

n. A metro rider who takes up too much space with his/her enormous coat, hat, bag, and wet umbrella.

HOLIDAYS

n. Deviation. Diversion. An excuse to eat, drink, and receive presents. Any weekday that you spend away from work. Your mom's evil way of ensuring you visit.

We work hard. Before we eat lunch (pizza) and after snacks (vodka), we work hard. In between researching (*Britney Spears did what?*) and investigating (*Paris Hilton did who?*), we work hard. After returning from meetings (H&M) and before leaving for appointments (Kirna Zabete), we work our asses off. (Note to the Boss: The preceding was meant to be humorous and facetious. At this very moment I'm working incredibly hard writing the Holidays chapter, which focuses on Christmas. I was Bat Mitzvah-ed, for Christ's sake. Working hard, indeed.)

The point being: we're exhausted. Oops, no, the point is: We love holidays (*all* holidays).

Sadly, we only get five days off a year: Christmas, New Year's, President's Day, the Fourth, and Thanksgiving. It may be possible that we get more than that. I didn't research this or anything. (In fact, I just remembered two more: Labor Day and Memorial Day.) And while that may *seem* like plenty, you must consider the holidays that we—shockingly—don't get off:

1. MARTIN LUTHER KING DAY: Is there someone we can call about this? The Reverend Sharpton?

2. COLUMBUS DAY: Now that's just unpatriotic. Un-American. Except to Native Americans, who probably don't care.

3. HALLOWEEN: Have you ever tried to take the subway to work while dressed as a Slutty Dog Walker? It's impossible.

4. THE DAY AFTER HALLOWEEN: Have you ever tried to come to work on the day after going out as a Slutty Dog Walker? It's impossible.

5. NATIONAL POETRY DAY:
We're not off this day
Though we're all fine prose writers
Dabbling in Haiku

6. MY BIRTHDAY: WTF?

The problem with getting so few holidays off is that they aren't all fun and games. A lot of holidays are just a different kind of work. And like all unpleasantness, it starts with your mother and a twelve-step program.

STEP 1. Admit you have a problem: You have to go home. Your mom hasn't seen you since . . . last week. Besides, if her "I miss you" guilt fails, she's not above hypothetically killing your grandparents. (*They won't be around much longer.*)

STEP 2. Plan the trip, which may include planes, trains, automobiles, and for one sad DailyCandy-ite, whose family lives in New Jersey, a ferry.

STEP 3. Meditate. It's going to take a Buddha-like calm to face Aunt Suzie, who likes to point out that since she last saw you, you've gotten paler and less pregnant.

STEP 4. Fight with your sister.

STEPS 5-10. Accept your mom's need to criticize all your life choices.

STEP 11. Make amends with both your sister and mother (*not* Aunt Suzie).

STEP 12. Return home, a shadow of your former self, with just six measly hours to sleep before work. All you have to show for it: a new iPhone. (Thanks, Mom, you're the best!)

And that's just Thanksgiving. Don't even get us started on Valentine's Day. Below are some words gleaned from Festivus and the rest of it.

BROWN NOSED REINDEER

n. An employee who starts kissing up right before Christmas bonuses are scheduled to arrive.

CRYDAY THE 13TH

n. The day before Valentine's Day if you're single.

The year: 2005. The date: February 13. The location: Murray Hill, the apartment of infamous hostess and ex-employee, J.C. That notorious night spawned Cryday the 13th. In an exercise in bonding, all the DailyCandy ladies (who back then could fit in an NYC apartment) organized the First (and Last) Annual Pre-Valentine's Day Pot Luck Dinner. The event's name was literal: Lily brought bacon-wrapped figs, Gwen brought a variety of cheeses, and Simone brought pot.

DREIDEL ROBBER

n. An adult who snags all the kids' new Hanukah toys but doesn't play well with others. *(My brother, the dreidel robber, is outside with little Tommy's new bike.)*

EGGSNOG

n. A makeout session that takes place under the influence of eggnog.

Ah, the Tech Boys (the only boys) of DailyCandy. It is a complete fabrication, a dastardly lie, a friggin' falsehood, that even one among us has made out with an elusive DailyCandyman after downing a few too many eggnogs. After all, we drink Scotch.

ERIN GO BRA-LESS

n. When you drink enough to take your top off on Saint Patrick's Day. *(One more green beer and I'm Erin go bra-less.)*

One infamous St. Paddy's, a certain editor had one Bushmill's too many and failed to notice that an extra button (or two) had opened on her shirt. A fireman kindly pointed it out.

HACK O' LANTERN

n. A really junky pumpkin.

HALLMARKETING

n. The outrageous marketing push that begins two months before each holiday, i.e., Halloween decorations in July, Christmas decorations in October.

HOLIBACK GIRLS

n. Women who are infamous for re-gifting. *(Grandma went all holiback girl, trying to gift me the very same bath soaps I gave her last year.)*

JEW-ISH

n. One who suddenly finds God (the Hebrew G-d, or as we call him, Yahweh) around the Jewish holidays. *(When Mary Katherine took off for Passover, we all knew she was Jew-ish.)*

JINGLE BELLES

n. The exposed cleavage of women who dress inappropriately at the holiday party.

LITTLE CLOWN OF BETHLEHEM

n. Someone who gets overly drunk at a holiday party.
See also: jingle belles.

This past Christmas, the holiday party was at a Karaoke bar. Lily slayed with her performance of "Nine to Five," sung directly to the Boss: "Want to move ahead/but the boss won't seem to let me/I swear sometimes/that man is out to get me." After that, we cut her off.

LITTLE WHITE LINE

n. The invisible divide between Labor Day and the start of September upon which white pants die.

MENORAH-TY

n. The kids at school who don't celebrate Christmas. *(The menorah-ty always knew Santa was a lie.)*

MISTLEHO

n. Someone who hangs around under the mistletoe, waiting to get kissed. *(She was such a mistleho at the company party that no one else could get any play from the accounting department.)*

MRS. CLAWS

n. A work buddy's wife whose steely gaze keeps her husband's female colleagues on the other side of the office-party dance floor.

PILL-GRIMS

n. 1. People who dislike Thanksgiving. 2. People who need an antacid pill after Thanksgiving dinner (i.e., everyone).

REIGNDEER GAMES

v. The domineering attitude of some zealots concerning the Christmas decorations. (*My sister plays such reigndeer games I refuse to decorate the tree with her.*)

ROUND YON VIRGIN

n. A severely overweight child relative who hogs all the dessert. (*I never even got to try Aunt Martha's cranberry squares—the round yon virgins charged the dessert table.*)

Each year, Heidi arranges for the office tree. She also orchestrates the decorations. She does not want your help. In her own words, "Not everyone has the Christmas sensibilities that I do." She's dead serious. And Southern.

SANTA FRAUD

n. One who suddenly finds God (and Jesus) around Christmas. *(Hannah's a Santa fraud, giving me her Christmas list right after temple.) See also:* Jew-ish.

SEXY SEAMSTRESS/ KINKY KNITTER

n. A girl whose Halloween costume is just an excuse to dress slutty.

A bunch of us were at a Halloween party last year. We couldn't help but notice that every girl's costume was a variation of Sexy Something: sexy nurse, sexy dog walker, sexy Disney character (*Aladdin*'s Jasmine, with her belly flaunting, is always a popular choice). We thought, why the ruse? So the next night at another party Simone decided to go as a whore. It was more honest.

THANKS-MIS-GIVING

n. The feeling you have about going to your boyfriend's family's house for Thanksgiving dinner. *(After his mom asked me when I planned on getting married, I had Thanks-mis-givings.)*

VIOLENT NIGHT, TROLL-Y NIGHT

n. The aftermath of the holiday party where a certain elf swills too much vodka.

ACKNOWLEDGMENTS

This book is the work of the entire DailyCandy editorial staff, a virtual hive of whip-smart friends and colleagues who take pleasure in making each other laugh hysterically (and occasionally cry like small children). Many of the words and definitions compiled here are the fruit of countless brainstorms over the years—the collective voice of more than twenty unique individuals.

That said, there are a few people without whom this volume would not exist. Miami editor Brooke Siegel managed the project beautifully, beginning to end, and wrote most of the sparkling, irreverent prose you'll read herein. After which Eve Epstein (editorial director, word guru, and *Battlestar Galactica* enthusiast) threw in her two cents. Dannielle Kyrillos contributed an enormous amount of her talent, as did Lauren Lumsden, Jasmine Moir, and Jeralyn Gerba. Huge props to the team at Virgin Books, notably Ken Siman, Ann Espuelas, and designer Jason Snyder; and to our agent, Andy McNicol at William Morris, for indulging our dumb questions and occasionally high-maintenance antics; and to DailyCandy's own PR wizard, Meredith Howard. Of course, we're nothing without Dany Levy, our founder, editor-in-chief, and resident visionary, who not only invented the DailyCandy lexicon but also had the good sense and abiding faith to realize what a great book it would make. And we are forever indebted to illustrator Sujean Rim for making everything we do—including this book—look beautiful. Finally, a big thanks to our CEO Pete Sheinbaum, who always has an opinion, to which he's of course entitled, even when we pay no mind.